DANCE IS COMMUNICATION

Understanding Dance Teaching through the Coach Gregg Teaching Method

Refined through two decades of
real-world Hip-Hop dance teaching experience

First Edition · April 2026

Gregg "PapiiBDS" Whitlock

Dance is Communication:
Understanding Dance Teaching through
the Coach Gregg Teaching Method

First Edition

Published by Bernice Publishing
An imprint of BigBsBDS, Inc.

Dance is Communication
Release Calendar

First Edition - March 2026
Author's 38th Birthday release

"I had to get this off my chest."

First Edition - April 2026
Easter Sunday release

*"Same information with minor edits.
Can you find them?"*

Table of Contents

Table of Contents

Dance is Communication

MOST DANCERS KNOW HOW TO DANCE

BUT DON'T KNOW HOW TO TEACH

How to Use This Book

This book presents the Coach Gregg Teaching Method and the Subjective Dance philosophy that dance is communication. Readers may approach this book from many different perspectives. Whether teaching, learning to teach, or developing their own voice as a dancer, readers can use the ideas in this book to better understand how movement, music, and creativity connect.

The chapters are designed to be read in order. Early chapters establish the philosophy behind the method, while later chapters explore practical teaching environments such as class structure, musicality development, and classroom leadership. Each chapter concludes with Teaching Reflection prompts. These questions are designed to help teachers consider how the concepts apply within their own teaching environments.

My goal with this book is not to create identical teachers. Instead, it is to provide a framework that allows instructors to develop their own teaching voice while maintaining awareness, structure, and responsibility in the classroom.

Key Terms and Definitions

The following terms establish the language used throughout this book. Some definitions reflect commonly understood meanings, while others describe concepts developed within the Coach Gregg Teaching Method through decades of real-world teaching experience.

SUBJECTIVE (Adjective): Based on or influenced by personal feelings, tastes, or opinions.

DANCE (Noun): A series of movements performed in rhythm with music.

DANCING (Verb): The act of moving to the beat.

DANCE STYLE (Noun): A recognizable approach to movement within dance characterized by its own techniques, rhythms, and cultural influences.

STAGE DANCE (Noun): Dance created for presentation to an audience, typically performed in structured performance environments.

STREET DANCE (Noun): Dance styles that developed outside formal studios in social and community environments.

DANCE SCENE (Noun): A community of dancers connected through shared styles, music, events, and cultural influences.

DANCE LANGUAGE (Noun): A dance style that serves as the root for other niche dance styles and stylistic variations or dance dialects. Each dance language contains its own techniques, rhythms, cultural influences, and approaches to movement.

SUBJECTIVE DANCE (Philosophy): A philosophy of understanding dance as a form of communication that recognizes the many languages, dialects, and personal interpretations that exist within the art form.

SUBJECTIVE DANCER (Noun): A dancer who expresses personal interpretation of music through movement with strong musicality, confidence, and awareness of one or more dance languages.

SUBJECTIVE DANCING (Verb): The act of interpreting music through movement with strong musical awareness, either by blending multiple dance styles or by expressing a single dance style while interpreting music outside that style's typical genre.

SUBJECTIVE DANCE STYLE (Noun): A movement approach that emerges from subjective dancing, merging both stage and street dance skill sets while emphasizing musical interpretation, technical movement, and personal expression.

COACH GREGG TEACHING METHOD: A teaching framework developed by Gregg "PapiiBDS" Whitlock for guiding dancers and instructors through movement, music, creativity, and culture while helping dancers understand dance as communication.

DANCE IS COMMUNICATION SERIES: A collection of books documenting the philosophy and teaching framework behind the Coach Gregg Teaching Method and exploring how movement can be understood, taught, and communicated across many creative environments.

The Coach Gregg Teaching Method (At a Glance)

Dance styles are languages. When someone asks, "What style do you dance?", it is similar to asking, "What language do you speak?" In a world of Subjective Dance, answering that question gets tricky for a dancer who cannot identify different dance styles.

Dance styles such as Hip-Hop, Ballet, Jazz, House, Contemporary, Tap, African dance traditions, Latin dance styles, and club dance traditions operate as dance languages. Just as people who speak the same language may sound different depending on region, dancers may express the same movement differently depending on their influences, experiences, and musical interpretation. Since dance functions as communication, a teacher functions as a translator.

The Coach Gregg Teaching Method organizes dance education around five guiding principles:

➢ Responsibility ➢ Culture

➢ Translation ➢ Character

➢ Freedom

Together the five principles create a balanced approach to dance education that combines technical instruction, artistic development, cultural awareness, leadership, and guides the decisions teachers make across many teaching environments, including:

➤ studio classes

➤ competition teams

➤ film sets

➤ solo training

➤ community dance programs

A Simple Class Structure

While every instructor eventually develops their own teaching style, many classes follow a similar learning progression. Teachers introduce an idea, give students time to practice it, and then place that idea into a larger context through choreography, drills, or performance. A structured session might include things such as:

➤ a consistent warm-up

➤ a clear progression of material

➤ expectations for behavior and focus

➤ time for questions or feedback

Structure doesn't remove creativity. Instead, it provides a framework that allows creativity to develop in a productive way.

Your First Class as a Dance Teacher

Many dancers experience the same moment at some point in their journey. A studio owner, camp director, or mentor says something like: "Hey, can you teach this class today?" Suddenly the dancer who has spent years learning movement is standing at the front of the room responsible for guiding others. This transition can feel exciting, but also intimidating because teaching dance is not the same as performing.

The goal of your first class is not perfection. The goal is communication. If students leave class understanding your lesson better than when they arrived, the class was successful and the next few pages are tips you can take with you to be successful from Day 1.

Prepare the Body for Movement

Before students begin learning choreography or technique, their bodies need time to prepare for movement. Many teachers casually refer to this process as stretching but preparation actually involves several stages. The body typically moves through a progression: Cold → Warm → Mobile → Work → Cool Down

When students first enter class, their bodies are cold and muscles are not yet ready for intense movement. A warm-up helps increase blood flow and begins activating coordination and rhythm. There are two common types of stretching used in dance training.

Dynamic Stretching involves movement-based stretches that take the body through a controlled range of motion. These movements help prepare the body for activity and are often used near the beginning of class.

Examples may include:
- leg swings
- lunges
- torso rotations
- controlled kicks
- groove-based mobility exercises

Static Stretching involves holding a stretch for a period of time. This type of stretching is commonly used after the body is already warm or near the end of workouts.

Examples include:
- ➤ hamstring holds
- ➤ split stretches
- ➤ quad stretches
- ➤ calf stretches

Teachers may choose to stretch at different points in class, or sometimes not at all. In some environments, dancers may already be expected to be warmed up and stretched before class begins.

Start With Something You Know

For your lesson, choose movement you understand well.

- ➤ a favorite combination
- ➤ a groove you use often
- ➤ a short choreography phrase you made
- ➤ a basic technique concept

Students benefit more from a teacher who explains a simple idea clearly than from a teacher who demonstrates complicated movement without explanation. Start with material you can confidently break down.

Demonstrate, Then Translate

When introducing movement, show it first. Students often need to see the movement before they can understand it. After demonstrating, begin translating the movement into smaller ideas:

- what the feet are doing
- what the upper body is doing
- where the rhythm lands in the music

Breaking movement into smaller pieces allows students to process the information step by step. This is the beginning of translation.

Watch your Students

One of the most important skills a teacher develops is observation. While students practice, watch their movement carefully.

Look for signs that students may be confused:

➤ hesitation

➤ inconsistent timing

➤ repeated mistakes in the same section

These signs tell you where your explanation may need to change. Sometimes a different demonstration or a simpler explanation can immediately improve understanding.

Adjust When Necessary

Even with strong preparation, not every class unfolds as planned. Students may struggle with a concept that seemed simple during preparation. In other situations, a class may progress faster than expected. Be flexible in your approach. If students appear disengaged, introducing a creative challenge, freestyle moment, or new exercise can reenergize the class.

Be Patient With the Process

Students learn at different speeds. Giving students time to practice helps build both skill and confidence. Remember that improvement often happens gradually. Having patience is part of being a great teacher.

Keep the Environment Positive

Students learn best in environments where they feel supported. Encouragement helps students remain engaged even when the material feels challenging.

Correct mistakes when necessary, but do so with the intention of helping students improve rather than discouraging them. A positive classroom environment allows dancers to focus on learning. They come to class to practice. Some attempts will look messy. Some movements will take time to understand. This is part of the learning process. Don't be afraid to be transparent and vulnerable in your own learning process.

Class Time Is Practice Time.

Teaching Is a Skill That Develops Over Time

Your first class might not be perfect. Neither might your second or your tenth and that's ok. Teaching improves through experience. Each class teaches the instructor something new about communication, structure, and how students learn. Over time, teachers develop their own approach to guiding dancers.

The Coach Gregg Teaching Method presented in this book is designed to support that process and has been tested for two decades with dancers of varying age ranges and skill levels. The chapters that follow explore the ideas that helped me build strong classrooms, communicate movement clearly, get results on set, and guide dancers toward achieving goals with long-term growth.

Chapter 1

Introduction

Why Dance Teachers Matter

Dance teachers play an important role in the development of dancers, artists, and communities. For many students, the dance classroom becomes a place where they discover confidence, discipline, creativity, and self-expression.

The Modern Landscape of Dance Education

Over the past several decades, access to dance education has expanded dramatically. Studios, community programs, competitions, social media platforms, and online classes have made dance more visible and more accessible than ever before. While this growth has created exciting opportunities for dancers, it has also created new challenges for dance education.

Many talented dancers have become instructors, but being a strong dancer does not automatically mean they were prepared to teach. Teaching requires a different set of skills: communication, structure, awareness, and leadership. At the same time, some instructors enter teaching environments with strong classroom management skills but limited familiarity with the cultural environments that shaped the dance styles they are booked to teach. Both situations can create gaps in the learning experience.

The goal of this book is not to claim that there is only one correct way to teach dance. Instead, it presents a framework through five principles designed to help teachers develop their voice as reliable teachers. Responsibility, Translation, Freedom, Culture, and Character. These principles are vital for teachers who choose to adopt the Coach Gregg Teaching Method.

Teaching Is a Different Skill Than Dancing

One of the most common misconceptions in dance education is the belief that strong dancers automatically become strong teachers. In reality, the two skills are related but distinct. A dancer focuses primarily on performing movement. A teacher focuses on helping others understand movement. This difference requires teachers to think more about how they approach dance.

Instead of asking, "How do I perform this step?" the teacher must ask, "How do I help someone else learn this step?" Teaching requires patience and observation.

Every student learns differently. Some dancers respond quickly to visual demonstrations. Others benefit from verbal explanations, rhythm cues, or repetition. Strong teachers learn to recognize these differences and adjust their method of teaching accordingly.

Subjective Dance
and Artistic Interpretation

The term Subjective Dance comes from my experience as a young dancer. As a teenager I dreamed of becoming a mainstream Hip-Hop choreographer but I noticed that the style of dancing labeled as Hip-Hop in the mainstream media did not look the way I moved nor wanted to move.

That created confusion. I began questioning if what I was doing even counted as Hip-Hop dance at all. It took time to learn that dance is communication and we all communicate differently. Dance is also art, therefore dance is subjective.

The philosophy behind Subjective Dance recognizes that dancers interpret music through their own experiences, influences, and personal movement vocabulary. Two dancers may hear the same song and respond to it in completely different ways. This difference does not mean one interpretation is correct and the other is wrong. Instead, it reflects the personal nature of artistic expression.

However, artistic freedom still requires honesty and awareness. If a dancer chooses to represent a specific style with historical roots, they should respect the foundations of that style. Creative freedom and cultural responsibility must work together.

STUDENTS DON'T NEED PERFECT TEACHERS

THEY NEED CLEAR TEACHERS THAT CARE

Chapter 1 Reflection

1. What qualities do you believe make someone a good dance teacher?

2. Which of the five principles (Responsibility, Translation, Freedom, Culture, Character) do you feel most confident in right now?

3. Which principle do you feel you need to develop further?

Chapter 2

Dance Communication 101

Before dancers learn choreography, styles, or techniques, they are participating in something more fundamental: communication.

Movement allows people to express rhythm, emotion, intention, and ideas without speaking words. In this way, dance functions as a system of communication similar to spoken language. Both carry a message.

Dance styles are the languages we speak. Movement forms the vocabulary. Rhythm functions as grammar. Groove shapes the accent.

Just as people communicate through words and sentences when speaking or writing, we also communicate through movement and music when we dance. Because of this, the role of a dance teacher extends beyond demonstrating choreography. Teachers help students learn how to communicate through movement.

Languages Within Dance

If dance itself is communication, then many of the styles we recognize today function like languages within that system. Examples include:

➤ *Hip-Hop*
➤ *Jazz*
➤ *Ballet*
➤ *House*
➤ *Tap*
➤ *Contemporary*

Each of these styles contains its own movement vocabulary, rhythm interpretation, cultural environment, and performance traditions. A dancer who trains primarily in one of these styles learns how that particular language communicates through movement. However, just like spoken language, the story doesn't end there.

Over time, dancers are influenced by different styles, communities, music scenes, and teachers. These influences shape how they interpret rhythm, movement, and performance. Ultimately developing their personal voice in movement.

My Personal Voice

I say I'm a Subjective Dancer because my movement style, dance style, or dance language adapts in the moment, especially when choreographing for specific dancers, and was developed through exposure to several dance scenes. When dancing freely, my style is a fusion influenced by Funk, first-generation Jersey Club, Hip-Hop, House, Dancehall, and Contemporary dance.

When I began teaching professionally, I accepted the title of Hip-Hop dance teacher, even though mainstream Hip-Hop still looked different from my style of choreography. I've always stayed true to my foundational style. Over time, my ability to translate movement expanded to teaching opportunities in Gymnastics, Majorette, HBCU dance, Step, and movement work with actors and singers. Ultimately, those experiences shaped the direction of my studies and led me to write this book.

Dance Dialects

Using a single dance language as the example in this book makes it easier to demonstrate how dance evolves through communities and how different dialects of movement develop over time. Therefore, Hip-Hop dance will serve as the primary example throughout this book when explaining how dance languages develop dialects, regional influences, and stylistic variations. This example is not meant to suggest that other styles do not exist with their own histories, cultures, and movement vocabularies.

Just like spoken languages develop dialects, dance styles evolve differently depending on the communities, cities, or dance scenes they're in. When someone says their dance language is Hip-Hop, that statement alone doesn't describe everything about how they move.

Two dancers can both identify as Hip-Hop dancers while still moving very differently depending on the influences they grew up around. These differences function much like dialects within a language. Music scenes, regional trends, social dances, and community traditions all influence how movement evolves over time.

As dancers respond to these influences, new variations appear and the language continues expanding. Some dialects even grow to be dance languages.

Examples of dialects and regional influences commonly found within the Hip-Hop dance language include:

> *Breakin'*
> *Lite Feet*
> *Flexn*
> *Jersey Club*
> *Baltimore Club*
> *Chicago Footwork*
> *Detroit Jit*
> *Memphis Jookin'*

> *Turfing*
> *Krumping*
> *Jerkin'*
> *Hyphy*
> *Commercial Hip-Hop*
> *Street Jazz*
> *Trend dancing*
> *And more*

This list is not meant to define every style or influence within Hip-Hop culture. It simply demonstrates how many variations of movement can exist within a single dance language. No single dancer, teacher, or book can claim to represent the entire language.

New dialects continue to appear as music changes and communities develop their own interpretations of movement and extended vocabulary. From my observation, some dialects from other dance languages have even bled over into the Hip-Hop dance language with some generations of dancers not knowing it.

For more about Hip-Hop Culture see Chapter 7.

Other Dance Languages That Influence Hip-Hop

Over time, dancers moving between scenes allowed ideas from dance languages to influence one another. Because of this, certain movements and concepts from other dance languages can sometimes be seen inside Hip-Hop dance dialects. For example, Funk and House are two dance languages that have had significant influence on Hip-Hop dancers and the communities that surround me. Each developed through its own musical environments and social spaces, while continuing to evolve within its own dance scenes.

House dance developed through club culture and underground music scenes centered around house music. This dance language emphasizes rhythm, groove, footwork, and improvisation within social dance environments. While many dancers participate in both Hip-Hop and House scenes, the two dance languages developed through different musical and cultural pathways.

Examples of dialects commonly associated with the House dance language include:

➤ *Jacking*   ➤ *Footwork*   ➤ *Stomping*
➤ *Lofting*   ➤ *Skating*   ➤ *Shuffle*

Funk dance styles developed through music scenes connected to funk culture prior to Hip-Hop and House. Funk music emphasizes groove, bass-driven rhythm, and musical hits that dancers often highlight through movement. These movement traditions formed their own vocabulary and technical approaches to rhythm, groove, and performance. While these styles are sometimes taught alongside Hip-Hop in studios, they represent their own dance language with distinct cultural roots.

Many dancers train in both Hip-Hop and Funk environments, which has allowed ideas from these traditions to influence one another over time. Because of this crossover, certain movements and stylistic ideas from the Funk dance language can occasionally appear within Hip-Hop dance vocabulary.

Examples of dialects within the Funk dance language include:

- *Poppin'*
- *Boogaloo*
- *Strutting*
- *Animation*
- *Robot*
- *Dime Stop*
- *Tutting*
- *Waving*

These dialects may be understood as vocabulary within a larger dance language or as full styles of their own depending on the perspective of the dancer, teacher, or community discussing them.

Why This Matters for Teachers

Understanding the difference between languages, dialects, and influences helps dance teachers communicate movement more accurately. Students often see dance online and assume everything belongs to the same category. In reality, movement traditions develop through many different communities and cultural environments.

A master of any given style has a choice, not an obligation, to teach. A teacher does not need to be a master of every style in order to introduce a dance language to students. However, teachers should make it a mission to become fluent in the language they teach before stepping into that role.

Teachers, dancers, and choreographers must also recognize that the dance world contains many different movement languages and influences. Approaching those traditions with curiosity, honesty, and respect helps us dance responsibly while still encouraging creativity.

Dance continues to evolve through the people who practice it. The goal of a teacher is to help students understand the language they are learning so the dancer can contribute to the evolution of dance thoughtfully.

Respecting the Language

When dancers choose to teach or represent a particular style, they are representing a language that developed through communities and cultural environments. For this reason, it is important for teachers to approach styles with awareness and honesty.

Misrepresenting a style without understanding its origins can create confusion and unintended disrespect toward the communities that helped shape it. Yes, dance has always evolved through interpretation and creativity. Both things can exist at the same time. Teachers should respect the cultural environments that shaped a style while still encouraging dancers to develop their own voice within it.

Code-Switching Through Movement

In spoken language, people sometimes adjust the way they speak depending on their environment. This practice is often called code-switching. A person may shift their accent, tone, or vocabulary depending on who they are speaking with.

Dancers do something very similar. A dancer might adjust their groove, movement quality, or musical interpretation depending on the music, environment, or audience. The core identity of the dancer can remain the same, but the delivery may adapt to the moment. This ability to adapt while maintaining a strong foundation is part of becoming fluent in subjective dancing.

As dancers develop deeper understanding of a movement language, their interpretation of rhythm, groove, and expression becomes increasingly personal.

Chapter 2 Reflection

1. What "dance language" do you most closely identify with right now?

2. What styles, communities, or influences helped shape your personal movement vocabulary?

3. How might understanding dance styles as individual languages change the way you teach movement to students?

Chapter 3

The Coach Gregg Teaching Method

Every teacher eventually develops a personal approach to guiding students. Some instructors rely entirely on instinct and experience. Others develop structured systems that help them organize their teaching strategies and communicate ideas more clearly.

I developed The Coach Gregg Teaching Method through decades of working with dancers across many different environments: production sets, dance studios, community programs, performance teams, competitive programs, and freestyle dance spaces.

Over time, one pattern became clear. The strongest teachers were the ones who understood how to guide students through the learning process. They knew how to communicate movement. They knew when to challenge students and when to support them. They understood how classroom environments affect learning.

Most importantly, they recognized that teaching dance involves more than demonstrating choreography. It involves leadership, communication, awareness, and responsibility.

The Coach Gregg Teaching Method organizes those ideas into a clear framework using five principles that teachers can apply across many different teaching environments.

The Five Principles

At the center of the Coach Gregg Teaching Method are five guiding principles. These principles help teachers balance technical instruction, artistic expression, and cultural awareness.

The five principles are **Responsibility, Translation, Freedom, Culture** and **Character.** Together, these principles create a system that allows teachers to guide students effectively while still leaving space for creativity and individual growth.

Responsibility:
The Foundation of Teaching

Dance teachers influence far more than movement. They shape how students approach discipline, collaboration, creativity, confidence, and more.

The way a teacher structures a class, communicates with students, and handles challenges sets the tone for the entire learning environment. Students observe not only what instructors teach, but how instructors behave. They watch how teachers respond to mistakes. They notice how teachers treat other students. They recognize whether the classroom is safe, focused, and respectful.

Responsibility means understanding the influence and obligations that come with teaching dance. Teachers must create an environment where students feel supported while still being challenged to improve.

View Chapter 4

Translation: Communicating Movement

A dancer may understand movement internally, but a teacher must be able to explain that movement so others can learn it. This process is called translation. Teachers translate movement knowledge into language, demonstrations, and ideas that students can understand.

This might include:

➤ introducing origin of the movement
➤ demonstrating movement clearly
➤ describing rhythm or timing
➤ breaking choreography into smaller sections
➤ using imagery and metaphors to explain ideas

Different students process information differently. Some students learn visually. Others respond better to verbal explanation or repetition. Strong teachers learn how to translate the same idea in multiple ways. If dance is communication, teachers function as translators who help students understand how to speak through movement.

View Chapter 5 for more.

Freedom:
Encouraging Creativity

Structure is important in dance education, but creativity is equally important. Students eventually need the confidence to interpret music and movement through their own artistic perspective.

Freedom within the Coach Gregg Teaching Method means encouraging dancers to explore movement while still maintaining awareness of rhythm, intention, and style. Creative exploration helps dancers build confidence and develop their own artistic voice.

Freedom does not mean ignoring foundations. Instead, it means helping dancers build strong foundations so they can eventually interpret movement in their own way.

View Chapter 6 for more.

Culture:
Understanding Dance Context

In Chapter 2 we learned that dance styles develop within communities. Music, environment, and social interaction all influence how the movements evolve over time.

Teachers who introduce dance styles into classrooms should have an awareness of the cultural environments that helped create those movements. This awareness encourages students to approach dance with curiosity and respect. Teachers must recognize both the historical foundations of dance and the creative forces that continue to shape its future.

View Chapter 7 for more.

Character:
Leading by Example

Technical knowledge alone does not make someone a great teacher. Character matters. Dance teachers get the best results when they demonstrate professionalism, discipline, and integrity.

Students look to instructors for guidance not only in movement, but also in how to carry themselves within the dance community. Teachers who model strong character create classrooms and students built on respect and accountability.

These environments encourage students to support one another while maintaining the discipline required for growth.

View Chapter 9 for more.

How the Principles Work Together

The five principles of the Coach Gregg Teaching Method aren't meant to operate independently. They function best as a system.

Responsibility helps teachers understand the influence they carry. **Translation** allows them to communicate movement clearly. **Freedom** encourages creativity and personal expression. **Culture** provides awareness of the traditions behind the movement. **Character** ensures that teachers maintain professionalism.

When these principles work together, they create a balanced approach to dance education.

Applying the Method

The Coach Gregg Teaching Method can be applied in many different situations, including but not limited to:

➤ dance studio classes
➤ competition programs
➤ community dance environments

➢ workshops and training programs
➢ performance preparation
➢ freestyle dance development

The environment may change, but the principles remain the same. This flexibility allows teachers to adapt their approach while maintaining consistent values in the classroom.

Chapter 3 Reflection

1. Which pillar of the Coach Gregg Teaching Method feels most natural to you as a teacher and why?

2. Which pillar might require the most intentional effort for you to practice in your classroom?

3. How might these five principles influence the way you structure your classes moving forward?

Chapter 4

Responsibility

Teaching dance carries influence whether a teacher intends it to or not. The moment someone accepts the role of instructor, they become a leader inside the classroom. Students begin looking to that person for guidance, structure, and direction. Many dancers do not initially realize how much influence teachers hold. They focus primarily on movement, choreography, or performance. But teaching dance involves far more than demonstrating steps.

Dance teachers shape how students approach discipline, creativity, teamwork, and confidence. The environment created by a teacher affects how students feel about learning, how they treat each other, how they approach challenges, and sometimes translates to the real world. Because of this, teaching dance requires a strong sense of responsibility.

Responsibility begins with understanding that you set the tone.

Role Models by Default

Many dance instructors never set out to become role models. They simply enjoy dancing or choreographing and eventually find themselves in a position where others want to learn from them.

The catch is, once someone steps into the role of teacher, influence becomes unavoidable.

Students often admire the people who guide their growth. Younger dancers in particular may look up to teachers as examples of what they want to become. Even older students observe how instructors behave and carry themselves within the dance environment. Some students observe everything a teacher does. They notice how instructors respond to mistakes, how they handle frustration, and how they treat different students in the room. If a teacher shows patience and discipline, students begin to mirror those behaviors. If a teacher shows favoritism, disorganization, or disrespect, students can eventually reflect those behaviors as well. Because of this, dance teachers must recognize that their actions communicate messages beyond the movement being taught.

Most of us have been a student or a mentee before and still are. Think about how and why you have your role models, whether they know it or not. Now think about who might be looking up to you. This doesn't mean teachers must present themselves as perfect. It simply means recognizing that leadership comes with influence.

Structure Creates Safety

One of the most important responsibilities of a dance teacher is creating a structured learning environment. Students learn best when they understand what to expect from their training session. A clear structure allows dancers to focus their energy on learning rather than trying to figure out what the teacher, coach, or choreographer wants from them.

In my experience, providing a warm-up routine that dancers can start on their own has produced the best results when building confidence with dancers who come from Ballet or Contemporary backgrounds and are being introduced to moving comfortably in Hip-Hop or Freestyle movement.

A teacher who creates structure helps students feel safe enough to take creative risks. That sense of safety isn't only emotional or psychological. It also includes the physical wellbeing of the dancers in the room.

Physical Responsibility

Teaching dance also carries a physical responsibility. Because dance involves movement, balance, and coordination, teachers must remain aware of the physical demands placed on their students. A responsible instructor pays attention to signs of fatigue, frustration, or discomfort and adjusts instruction when necessary.

Movements such as tricks, flips, or stunts can be exciting to watch, but they should be used with clear purpose and proper understanding. If a student can perform a trick without understanding control, timing, or placement, the teaching has not been fully developed.

Students often trust their teachers to guide them safely through physical challenges. Respecting that trust means encouraging growth while still recognizing the limits of the body.

As teachers continue to grow, so should their awareness of how the body functions. While not every instructor needs to be an expert in anatomy, having a general understanding of how movement affects the body can influence how material is taught, corrected, and repeated. For those who plan to teach at a higher level, exploring areas such as anatomy or physical therapy can provide additional perspective that supports both the dancer and the learning process.

Discipline and Encouragement

Responsibility also involves balancing discipline with encouragement. Dance training often requires repetition, correction, and patience. Students will make mistakes. They may struggle with coordination, rhythm, or confidence.

A responsible teacher understands that improvement takes time. Rather than discouraging students, teachers get the best results when they guide their students through challenges while maintaining high expectations. Therefore, students should feel supported, but they should also understand that growth requires effort and persistence.

The best teachers create an environment where dancers feel motivated to improve rather than afraid to fail.

Teaching Versus Performing

One common mistake among new instructors is assuming that strong performance ability automatically translates into strong teaching ability. A talented dancer may understand movement instinctively, but teaching requires the ability to guide others through that process.

Teachers must break down movement, observe student progress, and adapt their explanations when something is not working.

Responsibility means recognizing that teaching is its own skill. Dancers and choreographers who take on teaching must shift their focus from demonstrating their own ability to helping others develop theirs.

Understanding Different Teaching Environments

Dance teachers also carry the responsibility of understanding the type of environment they are working within. Teaching in a recreational studio class may require a different approach than teaching a competitive team, a community workshop, an audition, or a freestyle training environment because each situation requires different expectations and goals.

Sometimes the objective of a class is to help students develop general dance ability and confidence. Other times the goal may be preparing dancers for a performance, competition, or showcase.

Although this book focuses primarily on classroom environments, the responsibility of shaping a learning environment appears in many movement spaces. Rehearsals, auditions, film sets, and stage productions all rely on leaders who can create focused, respectful environments where dancers are able to perform at their best.

Responsible teachers recognize the purpose of the environment they are working in and adjust their approach accordingly.

Setting the Standard

Responsibility ultimately means setting the standard for the classroom. Students take cues from the teacher's energy, preparation, and expectations. If a teacher arrives prepared and focused, students learn that preparation matters. If a teacher values effort and improvement, students begin valuing those things as well.

Teaching dance isn't only about movement. It's about guiding people through a process of growth. When teachers accept this responsibility fully, the classroom becomes a place where dancers develop not only skill, but confidence and character.

Responsibility and the Method

Without recognizing responsibility, the other principles of the Coach Gregg Teaching Method cannot function effectively. Because of this, responsibility sits at the center of the teaching process. It reminds teachers that every class carries influence. How that influence is used ultimately shapes the dancers you teach.

Chapter 4 Reflection

1. In what ways do dance teachers influence students beyond teaching movement?

____

____

____

____

____

2. How can a teacher create an environment that balances encouragement with accountability?

____

____

____

____

____

3. Think about a teacher who influenced you. What responsibilities did they handle well?

____

____

____

____

____

Chapter 5

Translation

Many dancers understand movement instinctively. They hear a song, feel the rhythm, and respond naturally with movement that fits the music. For experienced dancers, this process can happen almost automatically. However, teaching requires something different.

A teacher must be able to translate internal understanding into clear instruction so that someone else can learn the same knowledge. This process is known as translation. A dancer may know how to move. A teacher must know how to explain that movement. This difference separates performing from teaching.

Dance as Communication

Just as language teachers help students understand vocabulary, grammar, and pronunciation, dance teachers guide students through movement vocabulary, rhythmic structure, and groove. Clear translation allows students to understand not only what movement to perform, but how that movement communicates within the music and style.

When a dancer understands a movement internally but cannot explain it clearly, the information never reaches the student in a usable form. To the student, the movement may appear confusing or random. This is similar to hearing someone speak a language you do not understand. The sounds may exist, but without translation, meaning cannot be communicated. A teacher acts as the translator between movement knowledge and student understanding.

Teaching Like a Dancer vs Teaching Like a Teacher

Over the years I've noticed that many dance instructors begin teaching while still thinking primarily like dancers. This is understandable. Most teachers start as dancers first or are choreographer driven, including me!

However, dancing well and teaching well are two different skills. A dancer focuses on performing movement. A teacher focuses on helping someone else understand movement. When instructors teach like dancers instead of teachers, a few patterns often appear.

One common example is demonstration without translation. The instructor repeatedly performs the movement and tells students to "watch again" or "copy it," but never explains what the body should be doing or how the rhythm works. Students who already dance well may figure it out, but many others are left guessing.

Another example is teaching the final product instead of the process. Instead of breaking a movement down into pieces, the instructor jumps straight to the finished choreography. Students then spend most of the class trying to keep up rather than actually understanding how the movement works.

A third example is ignoring the learning environment. A teacher who is thinking like a performer may teach the same way regardless of whether the room is full of beginners, advanced dancers, or children. A teacher who is thinking like an educator adjusts pace, explanation, and expectations to match the students in front of them.

At the same time, dancers must recognize that different environments have different expectations. In some professional and choreography-driven spaces, the goal is not always to fully analyze or perfect every detail of the movement. Sometimes the expectation is simply to learn quickly and execute the choreography as it is presented. In those situations, dancers often need to adapt and give the environment what it expects. Being able to learn from a variety of teaching styles is part of growing as a dancer.

These are situations I often discuss with my students when preparing them to learn from different instructors or perform well in auditions. Understanding how different teachers approach movement helps dancers adapt more quickly while continuing to build their own understanding of dance.

Explaining Movement Clearly

One of the most important skills a dance teacher develops is the ability to explain movement clearly.

Being able to perform a movement well does not automatically mean a teacher can explain it effectively. Many dancers understand movement through years of physical experience but may struggle to translate that understanding into words that students can follow. This is where the principle of translation becomes essential.

Dance teachers must learn how to break movement into smaller ideas that students can recognize and reproduce. Instead of simply demonstrating a step and expecting students to copy it immediately, effective teachers identify the key pieces that make the movement work. Sometimes this means describing body positions. Sometimes it means pointing out rhythm or timing. Sometimes it means connecting the movement to a familiar action or image. Clear explanation allows students to understand not only what to do, but also why the movement works.

Strong teachers learn to combine demonstration, explanation, and repetition so that students can gradually build understanding. Explaining movement clearly doesn't suddenly mean using complicated words. In many cases, the most effective explanations are the simplest ones. The goal is to make the movement understandable.

When teachers develop the ability to translate movement into clear ideas, students learn faster, frustration decreases, and the classroom environment becomes more productive. Clear communication allows dancers to focus on learning rather than guessing.

Avoiding "Gibberish" Movement

Imagine hearing a person speak a language using the correct vocabulary but placing the words in the wrong order. Technically the words are correct, but the sentence makes no sense.

The same thing can happen in dance. A dancer might perform movements that belong to real styles or techniques, but if those movements are placed against the wrong rhythm, groove, or intention, the result may appear confusing to dancers who understand the style. To them, the movement can look like gibberish. This does not necessarily mean the dancer lacks ability. It often means the dancer has not yet learned how the dance language actually functions.

Teachers play an important role in helping students understand how movements connect to rhythm, groove, and musical structure. When students begin to understand that relationship, movement starts to make more sense.

Multiple Ways to Explain Movement

Strong teachers recognize that students learn in different ways. Some students learn best by watching demonstrations. Others respond better to verbal explanation. Some need repetition and time to experiment before the movement begins to feel natural. Because of this, teachers must learn to communicate the same idea in multiple ways.

A teacher might demonstrate the movement visually, then explain the rhythm verbally, then allow students to practice the movement repeatedly until the concept begins to settle in.

If one explanation does not work, a good teacher finds another way to explain the same idea. That's how real teaching works. Translation requires flexibility. The goal isn't simply to repeat instructions. The goal is to help students understand clearly enough that they can perform on their own.

Translating Rhythm

One of the most important translation skills in dance teaching involves rhythm. Many dancers can move naturally to music but struggle to explain how the rhythm works. Students who are new to dance may feel the music but have difficulty identifying the structure of the rhythm.

Teachers often need to help students recognize the patterns inside the music.

One approach I use is helping students listen for specific sounds within the music that repeat consistently. Once those sounds are identified, I assess whether we need to focus on finding the beat, counting the rhythm, or exploring more advanced musical interpretation.

Teachers can guide students through this process gradually, helping students build awareness of rhythm rather than simply copying movement or being told what to hear. After providing these guidelines, I often see the best results when dancers are allowed to figure out what they hear and demonstrate it on their own through either counting out loud or demonstrating movement. This approach helps me understand the dancer's rhythmic awareness and musical interpretation.

For more on translating rhythm see Chapter 8: Musicality.

Adjusting Translation for Different Students

Not every student learns at the same pace. Teachers must learn to observe their students carefully. If a student looks confused, the teacher may need to change the explanation. If the entire class seems lost, the teacher needs to try a different approach, simplify the concept, or break it into smaller steps.

Translation requires awareness. The teacher must constantly evaluate whether students are actually understanding the material being presented. Teaching is not simply delivering information. Teaching is ensuring that the information is being received.

Translation Builds Independence

The ultimate goal of being a translator is helping students become independent dancers. When students understand how movement works, they become capable of learning and creating new choreography more quickly. They can analyze rhythm on their own. They can experiment with their own movement ideas. This independence allows dancers to grow beyond the classroom.

Instead of memorizing steps, they begin understanding how dance functions as a system. Strong teachers recognize that their job is not simply to create dancers who copy movement. The goal is to create dancers who understand and appreciate movement.

Translation and the Teaching Method

Without translation, even the most talented dancer cannot effectively guide students. With strong translation skills, teachers can help students develop both understanding and confidence. Being a good translator is the ultimate test for anyone applying the Coach Gregg Teaching Method.

Chapter 5 Reflection

1. Think about a movement you understand well. How would you explain it to someone who has never done it before?

2. What are different ways you could demonstrate or describe the same movement concept?

3. How can you recognize when students are not understanding your explanation?

Chapter 6

Freedom

Structure is important in dance education, but structure alone cannot produce great dancers. Dance is an art form, and art requires space for personal interpretation.

Within the Coach Gregg Teaching Method, freedom refers to the ability for dancers to explore movement creatively while still maintaining awareness of rhythm, intention, and style.

Students must eventually move beyond copying steps. They must develop the ability to interpret music and movement through their own artistic perspective.

Freedom allows us all to develop our voices.

Personal Interpretation in Dance

When multiple dancers hear the same piece of music, they rarely move exactly the same way. Each dancer brings their own influences, experiences, and instincts into the movement. Two dancers may hear the same beat and respond in completely different ways. One may emphasize the rhythm through sharp movements, while another may interpret the same sound through smoother transitions. Both interpretations can be valid.

This variation is part of what makes dance expressive. Movement is not always meant to produce a single identical result. Instead, dance allows individuals to express how they personally experience the music.

The Painter Analogy

My favorite way to understand the freedom in dance concepts is through visual art. When a painter creates a painting, they often have a specific idea or story in mind. The artist chooses colors, shapes, and textures to express that idea. However, when people look at the finished painting, each viewer may interpret it differently. One person may see a completely different story than the one the artist intended. Another person may focus on details that the artist did not consider important. The painting itself does not change. What changes is the interpretation. Dance works the same way.

A dancer may create choreography or freestyle movement with a certain intention. But when an audience watches that performance, each viewer may experience the movement differently. Some may focus on rhythm. Others may notice emotion or storytelling. Others may simply respond to the energy of the performance. This is the subjective nature of art and the root of the art of Subjective Dance.

Freedom is Subjective Dance

Many dancers feel confident expressing themselves through movement but may not identify with a single defined style. Others strongly identify with a specific style and perform their style across many different types of music genres. In many cases, dancers blend influences from several styles while responding to the music in their own way. The idea of Subjective Dance developed from these observations.

Subjective Dance describes a dancer using their personal movement vocabulary and musical interpretation to express how they feel a song should move in that moment. The movement may be choreographed or improvised. It may draw inspiration from multiple styles or emphasize one particular influence. What matters is the dancer's ability to bring the music to life through movement regardless of the opinion of others.

Subjective dancing does not dismiss existing dance styles. Instead, it recognizes that we all speak the art of dance through many different languages.

Freedom and Style Awareness

Freedom in dance does not mean ignoring styles or traditions. Many dance styles have deep cultural histories and technical foundations.

If a dancer claims to represent a specific style, they should understand the foundations of that style. However, dancers who are expressing their own interpretation of music may draw from many influences while still developing their own voice.

This balance between style awareness and personal interpretation is important for dance teachers. Teachers must help students understand that creativity is encouraged, but honesty about influences and knowledge matters. Freedom becomes powerful when it exists alongside awareness.

Freedom in the Classroom

Teachers play an important role in helping students explore creative movement. Students often begin dance training by copying choreography or repeating specific exercises. These steps help build coordination and technique. However, dancers also need opportunities to experiment.

Freestyle exercises, creative challenges, and improvisation activities can help students develop confidence in their own movement ideas.

When students feel safe exploring movement, they begin developing their own relationship with music. This process strengthens both creativity and musical awareness.

Freedom Requires Structure

Creative freedom works best when it exists within a structured environment. A teacher who provides clear expectations, organized lessons, and constructive feedback creates a classroom where students feel supported. Within that environment, dancers can experiment without feeling lost.

Structure gives students the foundation they need to explore movement confidently. Freedom allows them to build their own artistic voice on top of that foundation. The combination of these two elements is what helps dancers grow beyond imitation.

Freedom and
the Teaching Method

Within the Coach Gregg Teaching Method, freedom connects directly to the other principles. Freedom brings the artistic element into the system. It allows dancers to move beyond memorizing steps and begin developing their own relationship with music and movement. When students understand both structure and freedom, they gain the tools to grow into confident and expressive dancers.

Chapter 6 Reflection

1. How can teachers encourage creativity while still maintaining structure in a class?

____

____

____

____

____

2. What activities or exercises help dancers explore their own movement ideas?

____

____

____

____

____

3. When should a teacher guide creativity, and when should they step back and let dancers explore?

____

____

____

____

____

Chapter 7

Culture

Dance can begin with an individual idea, but styles gain meaning through the communities that share them. Music, environment, and social interaction all influence how movement develops over time. Because of this connection, teachers who introduce dance styles to students are also introducing pieces of culture. Understanding this relationship helps teachers approach dance education with awareness and respect.

The Cultural Roots of Hip-Hop

As far as I know today, Hip-Hop culture emerged in the early 1970s. Before Hip-Hop emerged as a recognized culture, many dance communities were already responding to the rhythms of Funk, Soul, and Disco music in clubs, social gatherings, and neighborhood parties. These musical environments encouraged dancers to interpret rhythm, groove, and musical dialects in creative ways. Eventually Hip-Hop DJs took control of the musical influence and dancers from these earlier music scenes brought their movement traditions with them.

The official birthday of Hip-Hop is credited to be August 11, 1973, when DJ Kool Herc played music for his sister's back-to-school birthday jam at 1520 Sedgwick Avenue, Bronx, New York. During this event, Herc introduced the breakbeat as he extended the instrumental breaks of songs so dancers can dance to the beat for longer periods of time. These break sections of music encouraged the dance language that eventually became known as breakin' and the dance pillar of Hip-Hop culture.

Language and Style Names

As Hip-Hop culture spread through media and global entertainment, some dance style names changed and/or expanded. For example, original b-boys commonly used the term breakin'. When the style became widely visible through television and film during the 1980s, the media often used the term breakdancing. Over time, both terms became recognized around the world.

A similar situation can be pointed out with the Funk & Soul styles of Popping and Lockin'. These styles developed as separate forms of dance with their own techniques, histories, and influences. As the styles spread, many people began using the phrase pop-locking to describe the visual combination of both styles even if wrong in translation.

These naming shifts illustrate how dance language evolves when styles move beyond their original communities. Teachers who understand these differences can explain them to students in a way that provides context rather than criticism.

Expanding Styles and Regional Movements

As Hip-Hop culture grew for more than 50 years, local music scenes and communities continued developing their own movement styles connected to the rhythms of their environments. These regional dance expressions often reflect the music being played in clubs, parties, private events, and neighborhood gatherings.

Since dance continues to evolve, the list of styles continues to grow. New sounds and new communities constantly influence how movement develops.

The Technology Era

The modern dance world is heavily influenced by technology. Online video platforms and social media allow dancers to view styles from around the world instantly.

Movements that once existed only within specific communities can now spread across the globe in a matter of hours. This access creates incredible opportunities for creativity and learning. Dancers can study influences from different regions, discover new music, and connect with communities they might never have encountered otherwise. This access also creates new challenges.

Since dancers can now learn movements from videos without understanding their origins, it becomes easier to borrow movement from styles that are not fully understood. Teachers play an important role in helping students navigate this environment responsibly.

Cultural Awareness

Dance teachers do not need to master every style that exists. That would be impossible. However, teachers should maintain awareness of where movements come from and how they are traditionally used. If a teacher introduces movements inspired by a particular style, acknowledging the source of that style encourages students to explore the culture further. This approach builds curiosity and respect for the culture in question.

Problems occur when teachers present borrowed movements as if they represent the full authority of a style without understanding the culture behind it. In the dance community, this behavior is one of the ways to catch a negative label like culture vulture. Avoiding that situation is usually simple. Do research and don't lie.

Teachers should be honest about their relationship to the styles they reference and never claim ownership of movements they did not organically create.

You can be inspired, but don't steal.

Creativity and Cultural Respect

Cultural awareness does not prevent creativity. In fact, many dance styles developed because dancers experimented with existing movements and adapted them to new music and environments. Innovation is part of how dance grows.

The goal is not to freeze dance in time. Instead, the goal is balance. Teachers should encourage creativity while still recognizing the traditions that shaped the movements being explored. This balance allows dancers to experiment without misrepresenting the cultures that helped create those styles.

Culture and the Teaching Method

When these ideas work together, teachers can guide students toward both creativity and awareness. Students learn not only how to move, but also how to understand the environments that shaped the movement. This combination helps dancers grow into artists who respect the past while continuing to build the future of dance.

Personally, I have never been the historian type of teacher. My focus has always been on successfully translating movement so students can understand what they are doing and why it works. At the same time, I recognize that the more I learn about a dance style, the better equipped I am to answer questions and lead with confidence.

Not every piece of history adds value to every teaching situation. In many cases, even things people treat as facts are debated within the dance community. Questions such as "Who created this move first?" are not always easy to prove unless the movement is clearly associated with a specific individual. For that reason, my teaching approach is simple. I lead with what I know.

Chapter 7 Reflection

1. What dance communities or environments helped shape the styles you practice?

____

____

____

____

____

2. How can teachers introduce students to the cultural context of dance without limiting creativity?

____

____

____

____

____

3. What responsibilities do teachers have when teaching styles that originated in communities different from their own?

____

____

____

____

____

A GREAT
DANCE TEACHER

MEETS STUDENTS
WHERE THEY ARE AND
GUIDES THEM FORWARD

Chapter 8

Musicality

Musicality is one of the most important skills a dancer can develop. At its core, musicality is the ability to recognize individual sounds and patterns in music then respond to those patterns through movement.

Many dancers initially approach music through instinct. They hear a song and begin moving based on what feels natural. This instinctive reaction is valuable and often forms the starting point of a dancer's relationship with music.

However, dancers who develop stronger musical awareness gain a significant advantage. They begin to recognize the structure of music rather than simply reacting to it. When dancers understand how music is built, they can anticipate changes in rhythm, emphasize specific sounds, and make intentional movement choices.

Feeling Music vs Understanding Music

Many dancers rely heavily on feeling when they move. Feeling the music is important, but relying only on feeling can sometimes limit a dancer's ability to analyze what is happening inside a song. Teachers often encounter students who can move well to music but struggle to explain where they are inside the rhythm.

Understanding rhythm in dance is similar to understanding grammar in spoken language. Grammar organizes how words function together, just as rhythm organizes how movement aligns with music. When dancers recognize rhythmic patterns in music, they gain the ability to structure movement with clarity and intention.

When Students Hear the Beat Differently

As teachers begin introducing rhythm concepts, they often discover that students do not always hear the beat in the same way. A common example happens when teachers ask a class to clap along with the music. Some students clap exactly where the teacher expects. Others clap slightly early, slightly late, or on a completely different part of the rhythm.

This does not necessarily mean the student lacks musical ability. It usually means the student is listening to a different sound within the music.

Music contains multiple layers. A dancer may be responding to a vocal accent, a bass line, or another instrument rather than the snare or clap the teacher intended. When this happens, the teacher's job isn't simply to say that the student is wrong. Instead, the teacher needs to help the student identify the sound being used as a reference point and then introduce another sound within the music that may help organize the rhythm more clearly.

Recognizing Musical Patterns

As dancers become more comfortable identifying the beat of the music, the next step is recognizing patterns within the rhythm. Most songs used in Hip-Hop, R&B, house, dancehall, and other rhythm-driven genres follow repeating musical structures that dancers can learn to anticipate. Phrasing usually follows repeating patterns such as two counts, four counts, eight counts, or sixteen counts. A clap, snap, or snare sound often lands on consistent points within the rhythm, commonly heard on counts two and four within an eight-count phrase. Other patterns may appear as repeating drum loops, basslines, musical phrases, or moments where the energy of the music rises and falls. Recognizing these patterns helps dancers understand not only where the beat is, but also when changes in the music are likely to occur.

Teachers can guide students to listen for these patterns so they begin to anticipate musical moments rather than reacting to them after they happen. When dancers recognize how music is structured, they gain more control over timing, accents, and transitions within their movement.

Discovering the Top of the Eight

Once dancers begin recognizing repeating sounds and patterns, teachers can guide them toward identifying the beginning of a musical phrase, also known as the "top of the eight."

Finding the top of the eight helps dancers stay aligned with the structure of the music. Students can practice locating this point by listening carefully to the rhythm and testing different counting patterns until the phrasing begins to match the music naturally.

This process often involves experimentation.

Dancers may try counting along with the music and adjusting their starting point until the counts align with the musical phrasing. Through practice, dancers begin recognizing these patterns more quickly.

Counting as a Tool

Counting music is sometimes misunderstood in dance. Some dancers believe counting limits creativity or prevents them from feeling the music naturally. In The Coach Gregg Teaching Method, counting is simply a tool. It allows dancers to analyze rhythm when necessary and communicate musical timing clearly during rehearsals or group choreography.

Counting does not replace feeling the music and you should train to move fluidly between both approaches. Dancers may count when analyzing rhythm or rehearsing choreography, then return to feeling the music once the structure becomes familiar.

In group settings, counting also functions as a shared communication system between dancers. Instead of verbally explaining every movement decision, dancers can communicate timing and structure through numbers and rhythmic patterns that everyone in the room understands. This shared timing system allows rehearsals to move more efficiently and helps dancers maintain synchronization during performances. The counts themselves are not the performance. They are simply a tool that helps dancers organize movement together.

Sign Language in Dance

Dancers often use movement to communicate with each other in real time. Hand signals, gestures, and physical cues can indicate timing, direction, spacing, transitions, or intent.

This happens across many dance environments, including rehearsals, performances, battles, and freestyle sessions, where dancers must respond quickly without stopping the movement.

In these moments, movement functions as a form of sign language within the dance environment, allowing dancers to communicate clearly while the dance continues. This concept can be explored more deeply in another volume of the Dance is Communication book series.

Dissecting the Music

Developing musicality requires active listening. Teachers can help students strengthen this skill by encouraging them to pay attention to the different sounds within a song. Drums, bass lines, vocals, and background instruments often create multiple layers within the music.

Dancers can experiment with isolating and emphasizing different sounds through their movement. One dancer might choose to highlight the drum pattern. Another may respond to vocal accents or background instruments. These choices allow dancers to develop their own interpretation of the music. When students begin hearing music in layers, their movement becomes more intentional.

When Dancers Rush the Music

Another common challenge teachers encounter is dancers rushing the rhythm. Students who are eager or excited often perform movements slightly ahead of the music. This usually happens because they are focusing more on completing the movement than on listening to the rhythm.

When this occurs, teachers can encourage dancers to relax, listen more carefully to the music, and allow the rhythm to guide the timing of their movement. Developing patience with the music helps dancers stay grounded within the groove rather than trying to outrun it.

Teaching Musical Awareness

Teachers should approach musicality as a process rather than a single lesson. Some students quickly recognize rhythm patterns, while others need more time to develop this awareness. Observation plays an important role here.

Teachers can use warm-up exercises or freestyle activities to gauge how well students understand musical structure. If a dancer struggles to stay aligned with the music, the teacher may introduce simple listening exercises to help the student identify rhythmic patterns. Over time, these exercises help dancers strengthen their musical instincts.

When I encounter dancers who have good musicality, the next level of individual dancer challenge becomes predicting and anticipating accents, sounds, and lyrics within the music by dancing to unfamiliar songs. Dancers with master level musicality can dance to anything at any given moment.

Musicality and the Teaching Method

Musicality connects strongly to the principle of translation. Teachers must translate the structure of music into ideas that students can understand. Musicality ultimately allows dancers to move without guesswork. When dancers learn to hear music clearly, movement becomes more connected, expressive, and confident. When a class finally hears the music clearly and moves together, a teacher knows the lesson worked.

Chapter 8 Reflection

1. How do you personally recognize rhythm in music when you dance?

2. What strategies could you use to help students who struggle to hear the beat clearly?

3. When might counting help dancers understand music, and when might feeling the music be more effective?

Chapter 9

Character

Technical ability may open the door to teaching opportunities, but character determines whether those opportunities continue.

Dance teachers work in environments built on trust. Parents trust instructors with their children. Studio owners trust teachers to represent their programs professionally. Students trust teachers to guide their growth responsibly. Because of this, character plays a major role in long-term success as a dance teacher.

Character includes the way a teacher carries themselves, communicates with others, handles challenges, and represents the dance community.

Students notice these behaviors. So do colleagues, studio owners, and other professionals in the industry.

Leadership in the Classroom

Teachers serve as leaders inside the classroom. Students often look to instructors for cues on how to behave, how to treat one another, and how to approach challenges.

A teacher who demonstrates discipline and respect encourages those same qualities in students. A teacher who approaches the classroom with negativity or disorganization may unintentionally create an environment where students lose focus and motivation.

Leadership does not mean controlling every moment of the classroom. Instead, leadership means creating a space where students understand expectations, share mutual respect, and feel encouraged to improve.

Professionalism

Professionalism is one of the most visible aspects of character. Professional teachers arrive prepared. They respect the time of their students and the organizations they work with. They communicate clearly about schedules, expectations, and responsibilities.

Professionalism also includes reliability. Studio owners and program directors depend on instructors who can consistently show up early, teach effectively, and represent the organization well. A teacher who demonstrates reliability quickly becomes valuable in any dance environment.

Of course, things sometimes happen that are out of our control. When this occurs, communication is the only thing left to save your professional reputation and the people who rely on you.

Reputation in
the Dance Community

The dance world is often smaller than people expect. Teachers, dancers, studio owners, and choreographers frequently interact across different cities, events, and programs. Because of this, reputation travels quickly. Teachers who demonstrate professionalism and integrity build strong relationships over time. Those relationships often lead to new opportunities. On the other hand, instructors who develop a reputation for being difficult to work with, disrespectful to students, or even having bad hygiene may find opportunities becoming limited.

Protecting one's reputation is not about avoiding mistakes. Everyone makes mistakes. Instead, it is about handling situations with maturity, honesty, and accountability.

Professional Boundaries in Dance Communities

Character in teaching also involves maintaining professional boundaries. Dance communities are often highly social environments, and instructors may find themselves surrounded by unwanted politics, gossip, or conversations that extend beyond the classroom.

Strong teachers learn to stay focused on their role as educators. Avoiding unnecessary drama and staying out of conflicts that do not involve their class allows teachers to maintain clarity and professionalism in their work.

Teachers may also encounter situations where students attempt to form relationships that extend beyond the classroom or work environment. While building positive connections with students is important, maintaining clear boundaries helps protect both the teacher and the student.

In my own teaching practice, I have found that separating my work life from my personal life creates a safer and more focused learning environment. Students benefit most when the classroom focus is clear and it remains a space dedicated to learning, growth, and respect.

Teachers who maintain professional boundaries often develop stronger trust with students, parents, staff, local organizations, and global organizations over time.

Personal Integrity in the Dance Industry

The dance industry can also present moments where instructors feel pressure to compromise their values in order to gain attention, opportunities, or professional recognition. Fame, competition, and public visibility can sometimes encourage people to prioritize status over character.

Strong teachers protect their personal integrity even when opportunities appear tempting. Remaining true to one's values allows instructors to build careers that are based on respect rather than reputation alone.

Students observe how teachers respond to these pressures. When instructors demonstrate honesty, discipline, and self-respect, they model the kind of character that students may carry with them beyond the dance studio.

The most respected teachers are often those who remain consistent in their values regardless of the environment around them.

Being a Role Model

Whether they intend to or not, dance teachers often become role models. Students pay attention to how instructors behave, both inside and outside the classroom. This influence can extend beyond dance itself.

Teachers may shape how students approach discipline, teamwork, and personal responsibility. Recognizing this influence helps teachers approach their work with greater awareness.

It does not require perfection. It simply requires understanding that leadership carries responsibility.

Character and Longevity

A dance career can come in many forms. Some dancers perform professionally for many years. Some use it solely as their therapeutic release. While others take on roles involving teaching, choreography, or directing programs.

Teachers who combine strong character with strong teaching ability often remain active in the dance community for years. Their professionalism earns respect from both students and peers. As a result, new opportunities continue to come.

Character supports longevity. It allows teachers to build relationships, maintain opportunities, and continue contributing to the dance community over time.

Character Within the Teaching Method

Character ties the five principles together. It ensures that teachers who adopt the Coach Gregg Teaching Method lead with integrity, professionalism, and respect for both students and the dance community. When teachers develop strong character alongside strong teaching skills, they create classrooms that support growth, creativity, and discipline. These environments help dancers develop not only as performers, but as individuals.

Chapter 9 Reflection

1. What behaviors demonstrate professionalism in a dance classroom?

2. How can teachers model strong character for their students?

3. What standards should teachers maintain for themselves when working with dancers?

CLASS TIME
IS PRACTICE TIME

Chapter 10

Classroom Environment

A strong classroom environment allows students to grow without fear while still encouraging discipline and effort.

Dance classes should feel welcoming, but they should also feel purposeful. Students need to understand that the time spent in class is valuable. The phrase I use to capture this mindset is simple:

"Class time is practice time."

The classroom is not a place where students are expected to perform their absolute best at every moment unless the teacher specifies it to be that type of atmosphere.

The classroom is where dancers experiment, make mistakes, improve, and develop confidence. When teachers create this type of environment, students become more willing to take risks and try new ideas.

Creating a Safe Space for Learning

Students develop best when they feel safe to explore movement without fear of embarrassment.

Dance training involves trial and error. Dancers must attempt movements repeatedly before mastering them. Without a supportive environment, students may become hesitant to try. A teacher's attitude strongly influences this atmosphere. Encouraging students, acknowledging effort, and maintaining patience helps build trust within the room.

A classroom where students feel safe often becomes a space where creativity and growth happen naturally.

Encouraging
Creative Exploration

Creative exploration is an important part of dance development. Students who only memorize choreography may become technically capable but struggle to develop their own artistic voice like a robot or clone.

Freestyle/improv exercises and creative challenges help dancers learn to trust their instincts. These moments encourage dancers to experiment with rhythm, movement ideas, and musical interpretation.

Teachers who incorporate freestyle opportunities into class help students develop confidence in their own movement choices. For many dancers, freestyle dancing or doing improv can initially feel uncomfortable. With practice time, it then often becomes the source for some of the most exciting moments in a dancer's life.

Innovation in Teaching

Teachers should not feel limited to traditional teaching methods. Creative instructors often develop exercises, games, obstacles, and challenges that help students practice specific skills in engaging ways. These activities can be designed to reinforce the goals of a particular class.

For example, a teacher might design a musicality game that challenges dancers to respond to different sounds in the music. Another exercise might encourage dancers to create short freestyle combinations based on specific rhythms. Another may challenge students' awareness of vocabulary in different dance languages. Obstacle-style challenges encourage dancers to move across the floor using different movement qualities or transitions. These types of exercises keep students engaged while still reinforcing important dance concepts and practicing.

Innovation helps maintain energy in the classroom while supporting the learning process. The goal of these activities is not simply entertainment. The goal is training.

When designed thoughtfully, games and creative challenges can reinforce the same skills that traditional exercises teach.

Reading the Room

Strong teachers constantly observe their students. Every class has a unique energy. Some groups respond quickly to new ideas. Others may require more time to understand concepts.

Remember, it is the teacher's responsibility to learn to read the room. If students appear confused, the teacher may need to simplify the explanation or break the concept into smaller steps. If students appear disengaged, introducing a creative challenge or freestyle activity may help reenergize the class. Reading the room allows teachers to adjust their approach while still working toward the goals of the lesson.

Balancing Structure and Flexibility

While adapting to the class is important, teachers should still begin each session with a clear plan. Planning allows instructors to remain confident and organized.

However, experienced teachers understand that not every plan will work exactly as expected. Sometimes a class progresses faster than anticipated. Other times students need more time to grasp a concept.

Flexibility allows teachers to adapt when necessary. The best teachers start with a plan and have a plethora of back-up plans so they can adjust when the situation calls for it. Understanding the principles of the Coach Gregg Teaching Method helps teachers make these adjustments thoughtfully rather than emotionally.

Helping Students Build Confidence

Confidence grows through repetition and experience. Students who regularly participate in class exercises, freestyle moments, and creative challenges begin developing trust in their abilities. Teachers play a key role in encouraging that process.

Training like this is valuable in many styles especially Hip-Hop, where a dancer's confidence is extremely important for translating their dance language successfully. When students feel supported, they become more willing to try new movements and push past their comfort zones. Over time, these experiences help dancers develop both technical ability and artistic confidence.

Safety Awareness

Dance is a physical activity, and teachers must always remain aware of the physical wellbeing of the students in their class. While dance training should challenge dancers and encourage growth, it should never ignore the limits of the body.

Teachers should pay attention to signs of fatigue, discomfort, or confusion during movement exercises. If a student appears to be struggling physically, the responsible approach is to slow down, adjust the instruction, or provide a safer alternative.

The purpose of this book is to focus on teaching philosophy and communication. It is not intended to serve as a guide to anatomy, conditioning, or injury prevention. Teachers who plan to work professionally should strongly consider continuing their education in areas such as anatomy, injury prevention, and physical safety.

Understanding how the body works can help teachers protect their students while still helping them grow as dancers. Responsible teachers care about both the movement being taught and the bodies performing it.

Chapter 10 Reflection

1. What type of environment helps dancers feel comfortable learning and experimenting?

2. How can teachers balance discipline with encouragement in the classroom?

3. What actions from a teacher can help students feel respected and supported?

Chapter 11

Teaching Scenarios

Even when teachers prepare carefully, every group of students brings a different combination of personalities, experience levels, learning styles, and energy into a room. Because of this, teaching dance requires more than knowing movement. It requires the ability to guide students through real situations as they occur.

Strong teachers learn to make thoughtful decisions in the moment. They recognize when to push students forward, when to slow down, when to provide encouragement, and when to reinforce discipline. These decisions shape the learning experience just as much as the choreography or exercises being taught.

Understanding common teaching scenarios helps instructors navigate these moments with confidence.

Virtual Classes

Some teachers primarily work virtually, but one of the biggest challenges I faced as a dance teacher came when COVID shut the world down. At the time, I was teaching weekly studio Hip-Hop classes with 109 students on my schedule. Suddenly, everything paused. Like many teachers, I had to figure out how to keep teaching when the classroom was no longer available in the way I knew it.

That shift forced me to adapt quickly. I had to find the right equipment, a workable teaching space, and a new level of comfort with leading class without students physically in front of me. Some classes were live, which meant I could still interact with students through video. Other classes had to be pre-recorded, which meant I had to think differently and anticipate questions, confusion, and timing issues before they even happened.

A strong teacher must be able to guide students clearly even when the environment changes. Virtual teaching challenged my structure, translation, patience, and creativity in real time. It also reminded me that virtual teaching adds to the longevity of the career of a dance teacher from the technology era.

Performance Environments

Different performance environments require different teaching priorities. In some atmospheres, two of the most common performance formats are recitals and competitions, and the purpose of choreography is very different between the two.

In a recital environment, the focus is often on celebrating the progress of each dancer. Every student in the class has spent time practicing the choreography and building the confidence to perform in front of an audience. For many dancers, the recital represents the moment where they overcome nervousness and demonstrate what they have learned.

For this reason, I like to treat recital choreography like a final exam for both the students and myself. Students practice what I teach, then demonstrate that work on stage confidently. As a choreographer, I care a lot about how my work is presented on stage. But, as a teacher, I know the recital moment is not about me.

Whenever possible, teachers should design recital choreography so that every dancer has the opportunity to perform the material they practiced. Even if a dancer performs imperfectly, the opportunity to complete the routine on stage can be an important part of their growth and confidence.

Adding reflection time after recital is a bonus.

Competition and performance based choreography often operates differently. In competitive environments, the goal shifts toward presenting the strongest possible performance for judges and audiences. Choreographers may adjust staging, formations, transitions, and performer placement to create the clearest visual impact.

These decisions reflect the competitive nature of the environment rather than the participation-focused goal of a recital. Understanding the difference between these settings helps teachers make thoughtful decisions about how choreography should function. Recitals often celebrate participation and growth, while competitions often emphasize performance quality and visual impact. Both experiences can be valuable when teachers approach them with clear expectations and leadership.

Teaching Beyond Trophies

Performance environments also introduce another important lesson: how dancers handle success and disappointment. Not every routine will win. Not every dancer will be selected for every role. These moments can be difficult, especially for students who may measure their success through awards or recognition.

Teachers play an important role in guiding students through these experiences. When handled thoughtfully, disappointment becomes an opportunity to teach resilience, discipline, and perspective. Students who learn that improvement, effort, and dedication matter more than trophies often develop healthier relationships with their training and let it carry over into life.

Teaching Different Age Groups

Dance teachers often work with students across many age groups, and each group may require a different approach to communication and instruction.

Young children respond well to clear structure, patience, and creative exercises that help maintain focus while developing coordination and rhythm. Games, movement challenges, and imaginative activities can help younger dancers stay engaged while learning fundamental skills.

Teenagers respond more positively to deeper explanations, musical discussions, and opportunities to explore their own movement ideas. At this stage, many dancers begin developing stronger artistic identities and benefit from environments that allow them to experiment.

Adults enter dance classes with a variety of motivations. Some seek technical growth, while others enjoy the physical activity and creative outlet that dance provides.

Teachers must also remain aware of the maturity level of the students they are working with. Music selection, movement choices, and communication style should reflect the age group of the dancers in the room.

Maintaining these standards helps protect the trust that allows dance programs to operate successfully. Students, parents, and organizations rely on teachers to maintain environments that are respectful, safe, and appropriate for the dancers involved.

Listening to Your Students

Teachers can improve their classes by paying attention to how students experience the learning process.

One simple way to gain insight is by asking students what they worked on or learned during class. Their answers often reveal how well concepts were communicated and what aspects of the lesson resonated most strongly.

Some students may focus on choreography. Others may mention rhythm, confidence, creativity, or movement quality. These responses help teachers understand how their instruction is being interpreted by the dancers.

Listening to students does not mean changing every decision based on feedback. Instead, it helps teachers remain aware of how their teaching is being received.

Maintaining Leadership

While student feedback can be valuable, teachers must also maintain clear leadership within the classroom. Not every suggestion or request should alter the direction of a lesson.

Students benefit from teachers who maintain structure, discipline, and clear expectations. Learning to focus, accept correction, and respect classroom standards are important parts of dance training. Strong teachers balance openness with confidence in their goals for the class. Students often respond best to instructors who listen thoughtfully but remain steady in their leadership.

Handling Different Skill Levels

One of the most common challenges teachers face is working with students who develop at different speeds within the same class. Some dancers may understand movement quickly, while others require additional repetition or explanation.

Strong teachers learn to support both groups without discouraging either one. This may involve offering simplified options for dancers who need more time while also providing small challenges for dancers who are ready to move forward.

When handled thoughtfully, mixed skill levels can become a positive part of the learning environment. Students who progress quickly learn patience and leadership, while students who require more time gain confidence through steady improvement.

The goal is not to rush every dancer to the same level at the same moment. The goal is to guide each dancer forward from where they currently stand.

Artist Development

Artist development is a different kind of teaching environment because the goal is not always to build a dancer in the traditional sense. Sometimes the person at the center of the work is a recording artist, performing artist, or actor whose main responsibility is not dance itself. Dance may only be one part of what they are carrying while they also juggle music, acting, interviews, rehearsals, travel, wardrobe, media, and performance pressure.

That changes the way teaching must happen.

In these environments, the teacher often has less time and less room to over-explain. The artist is usually the center of attention, which means the movement must support their performance, not compete with it. The goal is not always to make them dance like a trained dancer. The goal is to help them move with confidence, clarity, rhythm, and intention in a way that fits who they are.

Translation becomes extremely important in artist development. A teacher must quickly identify what matters most:

> what the artist needs to communicate
> what level of movement is realistic in the time available
> what will look strongest on that specific body
> what supports the music, camera, or stage moment

In some situations, the work is about simplifying movement without making it look weak. In other situations, it is about helping the artist repeat a few key moments with consistency until they feel natural. This requires patience, observation, and the ability to adjust quickly. An artist may be multitasking mentally even while rehearsing. They may be thinking about lyrics, acting choices, stage direction, wardrobe, stamina, or the pressure of being watched.

Because of that, strong teaching in artist development is not just about choreography. It is about communication, efficiency, and understanding how to bring out the strongest version of the artist under real conditions. The teacher must know how to translate movement into something the artist can absorb quickly while still protecting quality, confidence, and performance.

Chapter 11 Reflection

1. How might your teaching approach change when preparing dancers for a recital compared to a competition?

2. What factors should teachers consider when working with dancers of different ages?

3. How can teachers support students who progress at different speeds within the same class?

Chapter 12

The Professional Dance Teacher

Teaching dance can take many forms. Some instructors spend most of their careers working within studio programs. Others travel teaching workshops, lead community dance initiatives, coach competition teams, or mentor dancers within freestyle and battle environments. Many teachers eventually experience several of these environments throughout their careers.

Because the dance world is diverse, professional dance teachers often move between different teaching settings including studios, community programs, performance environments, and areas of the entertainment industry connected to recording artists and media production.

Understanding these environments helps teachers adapt their approach while maintaining the principles that guide their teaching.

Studio Teaching

Dance studios are one of the most common environments for dance teachers. Studio teaching often involves working with students over long periods of time. Dancers may train with the same instructor for months or even years, allowing the teacher to guide their development across multiple stages of growth.

This environment often requires patience, consistency, and strong communication with both students and parents. Teachers must balance technique training, creative development, and performance preparation while maintaining a structured classroom environment.

Because studio teachers interact with students regularly, they often become important mentors in a dancer's life. The influence of a studio teacher can extend far beyond choreography, shaping the confidence, discipline, and work habits of the students they guide.

Workshops and Guest Teaching

Some dance teachers expand their reach by teaching workshops or guest classes. Workshop environments often bring together dancers from different schools or communities for a shorter period of instruction. Because time is limited, teachers must communicate ideas clearly and efficiently.

Unlike studio teaching, where relationships develop over time, workshop instructors often need to establish authority in the room quickly. They must be able to introduce concepts, demonstrate movement, and guide dancers through learning experiences within a single class.

Workshops often emphasize inspiration and exposure to new ideas rather than long-term development. In this environment, a teacher's ability to communicate clearly and create an engaging atmosphere becomes especially important.

Community Dance Programs

Many dance teachers also work within community environments. These programs may include youth centers, school programs, cultural organizations, or independent dance initiatives. Community dance spaces often serve dancers who may not have consistent access to formal studio training.

In these environments, the role of the teacher often extends beyond movement instruction. Teachers may become mentors who encourage confidence, discipline, and creative expression within their communities.

Community programs also play an important role in expanding access to dance. Teachers who contribute to these spaces help develop new generations of dancers who may eventually continue their training in other parts of the dance world.

Freestyle and Battle Culture

Freestyle and battle environments represent another important part of dance culture. In these spaces, dancers develop their ability to interpret music spontaneously and express their personal movement style. Freestyling to some is also known as improv. Battles challenge dancers to respond creatively to music while interacting with other dancers in real time.

Teachers, dancers, and choreographers who come from freestyle or battle backgrounds often bring a unique perspective into their teaching space. They usually specialize in dance history, style dialects, extensive vocabulary, and creative problem-solving within movement.

Building a Reputation

Teaching ability alone does not guarantee opportunities. Professional dance teachers must also build a reputation within the communities they serve. This reputation develops gradually through reliability, professionalism, and the quality of the experiences teachers create for their students. Teachers who communicate clearly, prepare thoughtfully, and support their students consistently often earn the trust of studio owners, parents, dancers, and fellow instructors.

In today's world, teachers may also share their work through performances, workshops, or digital platforms that allow their ideas to reach dancers beyond their local community. The method used to build visibility is less important than the reputation built over time. Opportunities often come to teachers who consistently demonstrate professionalism and genuine care for the development of their students.

Expanding Opportunities

As teachers gain experience, new opportunities may begin to appear within the dance industry. Some instructors focus on choreography for performances, competitions, or entertainment projects. Others develop training programs, mentorship initiatives, or educational content that supports dancers beyond the classroom.

Teachers may also contribute to organizing events such as dance competitions, community showcases, workshops, or freestyle battles. These opportunities allow teachers to remain connected to the dance community while expanding their influence and sharing their knowledge with a wider audience.

The Professional Mindset

Dance teachers with a professional mindset respect the time and effort of their students. They communicate clearly with the organizations they work with. They remain aware of how their actions influence both the classroom and the broader dance community.

Professionalism does not require perfection. It requires preparation, consistency, and a commitment to improving over time. Teachers who maintain this mindset often build lasting relationships and meaningful careers within the dance world.

Professional Sustainability

Teaching dance as a long-term profession requires more than teaching ability alone. Professional instructors must also develop awareness of how they present their work to the world. Building a recognizable reputation within the dance community often comes from consistency, professionalism, and the quality of the experiences teachers create for their students.

Financial awareness is also an important part of sustainability. Understanding how to price classes, negotiate contracts, manage opportunities, and maintain financial stability allows teachers to continue doing the work they care about without unnecessary stress.

While this book focuses primarily on teaching philosophy, instructors who wish to sustain long careers in dance should invest time in developing professional habits, building their reputation, and learning the practical skills required to manage their work effectively.

Longevity in the Dance World

Dance continues to evolve. Music changes. Movement styles develop. Teaching environments shift as new technologies and cultural influences emerge.

Teachers who remain curious and willing to learn often sustain their careers longer than those who resist change.

Continuing to study movement, refine teaching methods, and stay connected to the dance community helps instructors remain relevant and effective. Longevity in dance education comes not only from skill, but from dedication to growth.

Develop a Teaching Voice

Every dance teacher eventually discovers that teaching is not only about explaining movement. It is also about discovering how to communicate ideas in a way that feels natural and authentic.

Two instructors may teach the same style of dance while leading their classes in very different ways. One teacher may rely heavily on demonstration. Another may emphasize verbal explanation and discussion. Some teachers connect with students through humor and energy, while others lead with calm structure and clear direction. These differences are not weaknesses. They are part of what makes teaching personal.

Many new instructors begin by borrowing ideas or drills from teachers who influenced them. This is a normal stage of development. Early in a teaching career, instructors often imitate the methods, phrases, and classroom structures they experienced as students. If you've never been a student in a classroom, that's ok. Remember to just start with what you know as a dancer.

Over time, serious teachers begin to notice which approaches work best for their students and which explanations feel most natural for them to deliver. Through experience, instructors begin refining their communication style and developing a clearer sense of how they want to guide a classroom. This process is the beginning of developing a teaching voice.

A teaching voice is not about personality alone. It reflects how a teacher combines their knowledge of movement, music, and classroom leadership to communicate with students effectively. Some teachers may emphasize rhythm and musical interpretation. Others may focus on movement vocabulary and technique. Some create space for freestyle exploration, while others guide students through carefully structured choreography. All of these approaches can be effective when the teacher communicates clearly and leads with intention.

Within the Coach Gregg Teaching Method, the goal is not to produce identical teachers. The goal is to help instructors understand how dance is communicated so they can guide students with clarity and confidence.

When teachers understand the foundations of movement, rhythm, culture, and communication, they gain the freedom to teach in ways that reflect their own strengths. A teaching voice grows stronger through experience. Every class taught, every question answered, and every challenge faced in the classroom helps instructors refine the way they communicate dance.

Like dance itself, teaching methods continue evolving through practice, reflection, and experience.

Continuing the Journey

Teaching dance is not a static profession. Each class, each group of students, and each teaching environment presents new challenges and new lessons. Teachers who remain open to learning often discover that their understanding of dance continues to evolve throughout their careers.

Becoming a dance teacher is not the end of a dancer's journey. In many ways, it marks the beginning of a deeper exploration of movement, communication, leadership, and responsibility.

The Teaching Method in the Professional World

The Coach Gregg Teaching Method applies across all professional dance environments.

Responsibility reminds teachers that their influence extends beyond the classroom. **Translation** allows teachers to communicate ideas clearly with dancers of different skill levels. **Freedom** encourages creativity while allowing dancers to develop their own movement voice. **Culture** helps teachers represent dance traditions honestly and respectfully. **Character** ensures that teachers maintain professionalism and integrity throughout their careers.

When these principles guide a teacher's approach, they create opportunities not only for their students to grow, but also for their own continued development as educators.

Chapter 12 Reflection

1. What habits or behaviors help a teacher maintain professionalism in the dance industry?

____

____

____

____

____

2. How can teachers prepare students for both studio environments and professional opportunities?

____

____

____

____

____

3. What steps might help you build a sustainable career as a dance teacher?

____

____

____

____

____

Chapter 13

Closing Philosophy

Dance is communication. Human beings use movement to express ideas, emotions, and energy that cannot always be explained with words. Long before formal dance studios existed, people were already using rhythm and movement to share stories, celebrate, and connect with one another.

Teaching is helping dancers learn how to understand and use dance in conversation. At that moment, dance becomes communication. This idea sits at the center of the Coach Gregg Teaching Method.

Since dance is also an art form, interpretation will always be subjective. At the same time, dancers benefit from understanding the cultural roots of the styles they practice.

Dance will continue evolving long after this book is written. New generations of dancers will create new ideas, reinterpret music in new ways, and continue expanding the culture of movement. Teachers who approach their work with curiosity and respect help guide that evolution in positive ways. They preserve knowledge while encouraging innovation. They support creativity while honoring the traditions that shaped the art form.

The work of teaching dance never truly ends. It continues in every class, every rehearsal, and every moment when a dancer discovers something new about how to communicate movement.

Remember...

DANCE IS COMMUNICATION
TEACHERS ARE TRANSLATORS

Final Reflection

1. What kind of dance teacher do you want to become?

____

____

____

____

____

2. How will the ideas in this book influence the way you guide and support your students?

____

____

____

____

____

3. How will you continue growing as both a teacher and a student of dance?

____

____

____

____

____

The Dance Teacher Code

Dance teachers hold a unique responsibility. The way you teach movement influences how students understand discipline, creativity, culture, and collaboration.

"Class time is practice time." - Coach Gregg

The following principles define the standards expected of teachers developing through the Coach Gregg Teaching Method.

---

1. **Responsibility** - Teachers influence more than choreography. Students observe how teachers speak, behave, and respond to challenges. Because of this, a teacher must approach the classroom with awareness and intention. Create an environment where students feel supported while still being challenged to grow.

2. **Translation** - Understanding movement is not the same as teaching movement. Teachers must be able to communicate ideas clearly so students can understand and apply them. Great teachers learn how to explain movement in multiple ways because every student learns differently.

3. **Freedom** - Dance is an art form built on expression. Teachers should encourage students to explore movement, interpret music, and develop their own voice. Creative freedom strengthens confidence and helps dancers grow beyond imitation.

4. **Culture** - Dance styles come from communities. Teachers should acknowledge the cultural environments that shaped the movements they teach. Respecting culture does not limit creativity. It strengthens the understanding behind the movement.

5. **Character** - Professionalism matters. Teachers must lead with discipline, integrity, and respect for the classroom environment. Students learn not only from what teachers teach, but from how teachers carry themselves.

Dance is communication.
Styles are the languages.
Movement is the vocabulary.
Rhythm is the grammar.
Groove is the accent.
Teachers are translators who help dancers find their voice.

INDEX

About the Author

Coach Gregg "Papii BDS" Whitlock, is a DJ, dance educator, actor, and choreographer. Originally from East Orange, New Jersey, and writing this book in Richmond, Virginia, he has spent decades teaching dancers through studio programs, community initiatives, competitive teams, and independent training environments.

Over the course of his career, he has guided thousands of dancers while emphasizing confidence, musical understanding, creativity, and leadership within the dance community. Coach Gregg is the founder of the Subjective Dance Club and the creator of The Coach Gregg

Teaching Method, a philosophy developed through 15 uninterrupted years of classroom experience teaching Hip-Hop to Ballerinas with clear communication and cultural awareness.

In addition to teaching and choreography, Coach Gregg remains active as a performer within freestyle and battle dance communities as DJ BDS. He also performs as an actor and dancer under the name PapiiBDS. His performance and media credits include appearances connected to Apple TV+, ESPN, GEICO, Virginia Lottery, Super Bowl LIX, and more.

Dance Is Communication represents the foundation of his teaching philosophy and the starting point of a larger series focused on developing teachers, dancers, and leaders within the dance community.

Papii's Blessed. Don't Sleep.
https://linktree.com/papiibds
@CoachGreggChoreo
@PapiiBDS

*PERSISTENCE OVER
EVERYTHING*
DON'T QUIT